GRIT. GRIND. GROW!

A Guide To Conquering Career Transition

ALEXIS (LEX) R. BROWN II

FORTIPHI, LLC

https://fortiphi.co

Testimonials

Grit. Grind. Grow! A Guide to Conquering Career Transition by Alexis (Lex) R. Brown II is a career guide and a motivational business career book written to help you take control of your career like an entrepreneur, thereby empowering and preparing you to secure and take advantage of the biggest and most juicy business deals, quickly, frequently, and consistently with the help of your brand strategies, human interaction skills and an elite list of references.

The book teaches by giving detailed and practical guidelines and steps to get through the frustrating career transition period you might be passing through and onto a bigger platform. What I found really fascinating about the book were the numerous tips to help any struggling, confused, or financially handicapped businessman or woman recover or start afresh in the business world of today. The author wrote series of concise and easy-to-digest tips for both high school graduates and college graduates as well. I found these tips helpful as I picked up a few things I would need if I decide to start up a business of my own.

Another part of the book I was very much interested in was the author's brief tale about his financial struggles despite being well qualified to secure a job without much fuss. The fact that he was able to forge ahead despite the disappointments and hurtful encounters was a source of inspiration. His inspirational quotes littered throughout the book inspired me. I came to learn that giving up was not an option. If you ever feel yourself losing control of any situation you find yourself in, stand still, think, analyze your options, and move forward again! This was what I liked most about the book.

A sour part of the book for me was the numerous websites and links which took a large chunk of the pages. Don't get me wrong, I believe they are an essential part of the formation of the book but I felt that it took away the sting from the book. I would have preferred to have more pages of the dos and don'ts in the business world than to have numerous websites for a particular reference point or topic. This was what I disliked most about the book.

Notwithstanding, the book is thoroughly fantastic in every way. It was grammatically edited. Although I noted only one grammatical error in the entire book, it took nothing away from the beauty of the message the book passed on. Because of this, I would rate *Grit. Grind. Grow! A Guide to Conquering Career Transition* by Alexis (Lex) R. Brown II, a **4 out of 4 stars**. I recommend this book to people struggling financially and those looking for tips on how to break free from the shackles of business misery.

- OnlineBookClub.org

TABLE OF CONTENTS

INTRODUCTION

After seven good years in the United States Air Force, I decided it was time to venture out into civilian life. Armed with a bachelor's degree in business, a strong technical background, and numerous accounts of leadership experience, I just knew I was guaranteed immediate success. I had a solid resume, so I said to myself "yep, I'm an undeniable candidate for hire". Nearly two years of transformational transition proved that statement so wrong - but only in the beginning, before I learned, adapted, and overcame.

By the grace of The Most High God, and with the love and support of my family, I endured heaps of no's, maybes, low-ball offers, and false-starts. I exhausted my Post 9/11 G.I. Bill benefits to pursue additional credentials, but also to sustain shelter and provisions for my family using the housing allowance. I even got laid off for the first time ever in my life, after just a few weeks once I did finally land a position! With my head hanging and my shoulders slumped, I often paid bills late using unemployment insurance, and bought groceries with food stamps. Up to that point, I'd worked a job continuously since the age of thirteen.

Food stamps and unemployment were the absolute last resort, and I'd reached my last.

Yet, joy comes in the morning, because the sun still rises after dark. Those two years morphed me into a much better version of myself. I gleaned a lot of strategies, tactics, and techniques from them that lead me to the rewarding circumstances I am blessed with today. In this book I will share much of what I learned with you, in hopes that it will help you embrace your purpose, take meaningful action, and achieve the results you seek. I'm happy to say that I've conquered my career transition, and I know that this book will help you conquer yours too.

This book is certainly for anyone who's seeking the insight and solutions being shared here. However, I did write this book having six target groups in mind:

1. **Transitioning Military Veterans:** Every year over 250,000 armed forces service members leave the military to reintegrate into the civilian public and private-sector workforces. Nearly 90 percent relocate to another area; many of whom also take a long-delayed vacation to celebrate joining the civilian world and give careful consideration to what's next. I'm a Vet, and I've been down this road. If you're also in this category, I'm confident this book will speak to you in some way.

2. **Military Spouses:** Over 93 percent of all military spouses are women, and women already have several unique factors to face in their career and business paths. Combine that with the fact that Military families are continually moving from base to base, causing spouses to frequently have to transfer jobs or seek new employment opportunities. This frequently makes landing great jobs challenging for them. My book addresses being dynamic and adaptable for such reasons.

3. **Unemployed Citizens:** According to World Bank and the US Bureau of Labor Statics, the US Unemployment Rate post COVID-19 is hovering around 6.7% - this is a captive audience awaiting great content such as Grit Grind Grow to motivate, inspire, and guide them on their journeys to achieving gainful employment. If you're in this group at the moment, stay strong and be encouraged - tough times don't last, but tough people who read books like this one do :)

4. **Recent College Graduates:** Usually somewhere from 18 to 30 years of age, this group is still assessing their professional and personal directions for life. This book is written to help streamline that life phase.

5. **Professionals of Color:** As a Black man, I've had my fair share of opportunities where I sensed that bias regarding my cultural identity may have prevented me as the most viable candidate from being otherwise selected. That's why I've devised a few tactics to mitigate this issue, particularly when I talk about treating job hunting and interviewing as a sales process later in the book.

6. **Seasoned Professionals (Ages 50+):** If you're 50 and up, you may feel a bit out of sorts in what's seeming to be a very youth-biased technology-driven work culture. However, your years of wisdom aren't holding you back. In fact, it's an obvious advantage in most cases. However, your willingness to learn and your desire to change and grow are where the impact really is. Allow me to elaborate a few pages from now.

If you're not associated with one of the six groups I just mentioned, please stick with me and continue reading, because you deserve great content and even better results, too!

GRIT

Resilience

You might be reading this book at a time of personal adversity, brought on by involuntary change (such as being laid off due to the very annoying COVID-19 pandemic). Or, maybe you chose change, but you're not yet seeing the positive results. If so, I hope you understand that you are NOT your circumstances. We all endure hurdles and hardships throughout our lifetimes. Loss of employment, medical setbacks, car repossessions, evictions, bankruptcies, etc. – these are all too common unfortunate occurrences across society.

Although challenging, inconvenient, and often frustrating, your transition journey can and should strengthen you, humble you, grow you, and prepare you for the new roles, responsibilities, relationships, and rewards that lay ahead. You must persevere. You can and will recover, and any material possessions you may have lost can be restored to you.

One particular concept that will help awaken your force within is resilience. According to the American Psychological Association (APA), resilience is defined as the process of adapting well in the face of adversity, trauma, tragedy, threats, or significant sources of stress. It is essentially "bouncing back" from difficult experiences. In such a volatile, unrelenting, ambiguous economic climate, no asset is more vital than resilience.

What's great about resilience is that you can continue to build it up and strengthen it. It's something you've got to work on consistently, just like hitting the gym and working out to stay in shape. Sometimes resilience requires some renewing and refreshing. Maintaining great resilience can help protect us from depression, anxiety, and other mental health conditions. It can also offset physical illness and injury. With that said, before we go any further, here are four simple ways to build and maintain resilience on your transition journey:

Keep Things in Proper Perspective. Always remember that life goes in cycles. This means that any negative experience you may have can and should be only temporary. During those times of adversity, count your blessings. Look at everything and everyone positive around you, and appreciate the little things. This should help keep you balanced and hope-filled.

Make Meaningful Connections. As much as it is within your control, maintain a strong support system. This is your base for survival in life, and it requires as much from you as you demand from it. Bond with family, friends, and close associates on a regular basis. Make frequent phone or video calls. Write thoughtful text messages and emails. Get out and about for a shared breakfast, lunch, or coffee. Whatever it takes, just keep nurturing those key relationships.

Beyond your support system, build bridges through new connections to get where you aspire to be, even if the bridges are only virtual ones.

Take Care of Yourself. It is wise to maintain an active physical fitness routine, to care for your one and only body. Just as important is the state of your mind and spirit, which can benefit from active prayer, meditation, yoga, or whatever form of inner-exercise you deem best for you (to me, prayer is the most powerful of all). Although it takes a lot of effort to conquer transition, it's also very necessary to relax on occasion. Finishing a good book or an intriguing series on Netflix can provide a much needed mental escape from the day-to-day hustle and grind. Allowing yourself to relax will help prevent you from feeling burned out.

Volunteer. Volunteering will keep you humble, grateful, grounded, and level-headed, regardless of any struggles you might experience during times of transition. As the old saying goes, "do unto others as you want done unto you". Give, and your hand is open to receive. But that's beside the point. Helping others is great for the heart and soul. You can even pick up new and valuable skills through volunteering. And, you never know who you might run into that shares a passion for the same causes you volunteer for.

You're reading this book, so to me that means your resilience is already evident. Why? Because you're actively seeking ways to persevere in life, in spite of any setbacks. In fact, "resilient" should be listed as a keyword on your resume, and you should absolutely talk it up as one of your core strengths during interviews.

Get Organized

Okay, it's time to collect your thoughts, gather a new batch of confidence, and start organizing the necessary tools and resources that you, as a bona fide conqueror, will need. More than likely, there's quite a bit of data concerning you floating around in the digital time-space continuum. Leave nothing to the unknown, and don't disregard the slightest detail.

Your first order of business is to control your own digital footprint.

Understand the user policies of all social networks that you exist on, and take the time to adjust your privacy settings accordingly. If anybody tags you in a photo, you should configure your settings to alert you immediately and request your permission for your name to be tagged. Always ask yourself how the image will reflect on present and future opportunities. The same goes for any post tagged to you in general. For instance, on Facebook no one should be able to post anything on your wall or timeline without you first having the chance to review it, and then approving or disapproving it.

I also highly recommend that you use the same exact profile picture across each and every one of your social media profiles, for consistency and to become easy to recognize across platforms. This limits confusion with other individuals who share the same or similar name as you, or who may have the same or similar headline, job title, or any other related information. Your chosen profile picture needs to be taken fairly recently, so that people can find you easily after networking events, and so that hiring personnel recognize you when you show up for an interview (because they will have of course checked you out online ahead of time).

One of the most powerful moves you can make is to distinguish yourself from your competitors through personal branding. Competition on many levels is pretty fierce, and all for seemingly scarce opportunities. It's clearly not enough to have a resume and a cover letter. You have to be visible and actively engaged on social media. You also need a strategic plan, with a persistent approach to managing your personal brand across a variety of platforms. Another critical key to personal brand management success in this digitized world is human interaction.

It's still vital to get out and shake some hands, or to at least get on the phone and hold some compelling conversations.

Without a doubt, conquering your career transition requires a personal brand breakthrough. Your personal brand includes but is not limited to the following factors:

Reputation – what do your peers, subordinates, and leaders think and say about you?

Buy-In – do you believe in yourself enough to convince others? What supporters do you have that truly believe in you and your personal brand?

Education – be it a four-year college degree or a short-term certification, education and training is a key asset to always build upon throughout life. Make yourself as marketable as possible by ensuring that your education and training align with your career and business goals

Affiliations – are you connected to organizations that are relevant to your industry and your professional goals?

Knowledge Base – spend every spare minute that you can to become a subject matter expert/guru in something that you're passionate about. It's great to be a jack of all trades, but you should specialize in something also

Strengths & Weaknesses – perform a S.W.O.T. Analysis (Strengths, Weaknesses, Opportunities and Threats)

Resources – get your arsenal together, including but not limited to: business cards; an online resume/CV; a premium LinkedIn account; and any other resource that will help your personal brand be strong

Online Presence – you should be present on every virtual platform that could possibly generate leads (meaning potential employers or significant contacts)

Growth Potential – how much more could you still learn and do? What can you act on immediately?

Honors – awards, recognition and accomplishments are important to brag a bit about when it comes to your social media profiles, your resume, your blog, and definitely during interviews

Here are a few simple strategies to help boost your personal brand immediately:

Think like an entrepreneur, and treat networking as marketing. Who, what, and where are you targeting your networking efforts? We'll get into more detail on this during chapter three

Handle interviewing as if you're a Sales Representative. Understand that you are selling both a product and a service – you as the talent are the product, and your labor and productivity are the service. We'll do a deep dive in chapter three

Use personal-brand business cards as an easy prompt for your elevator pitch. Yes, you need an impressive set of business cards to signify your personal brand, and to help you out when people ask, "who the hell are you, and what exactly do you do?" What should be on your cards? Obviously, your name and contact information. Also, include your LinkedIn profile URL. Tech-it-up a bit with a custom QR Code (you can create one for free at http://www.qr-code-generator.com/), directed at your LinkedIn profile for easy mobile device access. Add in some abbreviations next to or under your name (i.e. MBA, PMP, ITIL, CCNA, etc.) for significant degrees and certifications that apply to you and hold weight in your target field

Automate your brand management plan with a weekly schedule. This is most effective if you're not online 24/7 tweeting or posting every miscellaneous detail of your life. Commit to managing at least one platform per day, this way you won't get overwhelmed or fall into the trap of oversharing

Example:

Monday: On LinkedIn, 'like' an interesting article related to your field, and 'share' it with your commentary added for context. Then, skim your profile for any needed tweaks

Tuesday: On Twitter, tweet about a networking event you're attending, "#SomethingTrendy" at folks or companies relevant to the tweet

Wednesday: On LinkedIn, find/join relevant groups; post some of your thoughts within group discussions; connect with recruiters and like-minded people; follow companies you're interested in working with; connect others and help someone else out; update your profile, and maybe even send an InMail or two

Thursday: Learn something new via FreeCodeCamp.org, Udemy, Salesforce Trailhead, Coursera, etc. Due to all of the freemium education and training available online these days, there's no excuse to not take advantage and expand your horizons. Go for in-demand knowledge bases and skill sets like data analytics, SQL, Python, Machine Learning, and much more. Such learning will keep you growing, confident, relevant, and primed for whatever opportunities will come your way

Friday: On Facebook, post something motivational, such as how awesome your week's been. "Like" a few light-hearted posts that are aligned to your personality. You can even share a funny video (but keep it appropriate so that you don't damage your online reputation). Facebook should be the platform for the "Everyday YOU" to shine through

Along with the above brand management strategies, I can't emphasize enough the importance of old fashioned human interaction. Shaking hands and making phone calls will open up more doors than just being one virtual fish in a vast digital ocean. Put a voice and a face to your name.

Level Set & Connect

You should definitely try and manage control of the results of any vetting conducted by potential employers as much as you possibly can. We've already talked about controlling your digital footprint. Now we need to control who speaks on your behalf, so that you have a stronger influence on what is said about you when you're not present in the conversation. Successful careers and businesses are built through good relationships, so hopefully you already have a few good relationships in place.

Having credible references initiates some of those vital connections, by almost instantly helping you establish trust and validity. Your professional references should be strategically compiled with a diverse roster of contacts, ones whom you actually stay in touch with. Maintaining good references is evidence of good communication skills, and says that you're a well-respected and a likeable candidate. You'd do well to choose your references according to five vital categories: Mentors; Bosses; Clients; Peers; and Friends.

Be sure that all references in all of these categories are well informed of your intentions, and that they are properly prepared to respond when you include them as a reference. These are the five references you need in order to set the level of trustworthy and beneficial communication high during the hiring process:

1. **The Mentor.** A mentor reference should be very familiar with your personal vision and career goals, and should be willing to provide you with a letter of recommendation upon request. Mentors guide and counsel you, and understand how you respond to coaching. My mentor references help validate my preparedness to take effective action in the roles that I compete for. They publicly emphasize my strengths, but privately coach me on my weaknesses. They point me in the direction of opportunity, and warn me away from potential threats. The best mentor references are savvy promoters and powerful connectors

2. **The Former Boss or Direct Supervisor.** It is so important to make an amicable departure from every professional situation. Do not burn your bridges. If you've burned some already, then start making repairs immediately. Why? Because, in almost every potential employment scenario, your last supervisor is a primary person of interest. They know your roles and responsibilities well, since they managed the execution and fulfillment of them. Your last employer has a heavy influence on your professional pursuits. Even if you're released from a job based on unsatisfactory performance, this reference is still necessary and can still be used in your favor

3. **The Client.** Listing a client as a reference can provide a potential employer with testimony of your deliverables. Whatever outcomes result from your productivity (i.e. software code, website designs, photographs, sales revenue,

manufactured products, project management, etc.), clients are probably the most reputable voice for feedback. The client is primarily concerned with the scope, quality, and timeliness of whatever it is that you do as a professional. I really lean on my clients for references because they are the best proof that I can produce satisfactory results on a consistent basis

4. **The Peer.** The peer reference is your character witness, and should vouch for your interpersonal skills. This is someone who's been present during your day-to-day mode of operation. He or she can speak to your leadership potential, how you engage with others in the work environment, how you promote organizational culture, and how you function when under stress. My peer references speak of me as a team player, a motivator, and as someone that they enjoy working with on a regular basis

5. **The Personal History Buff a.k.a. The Old Friend.** This is the "true friend" reference, the person who knows your origins, how hard you work, and how far you've come already. My true friend references are able to share stories of trial and tribulation transformed into achievement and success. They know how I treat my wife, my kids, my mother, my siblings, and even my neighbors. They can attest to my continual progression. They might also share a funny story or two, just to lighten the atmosphere and give insight to who I am outside of work (in a positive, favorable light of course)

From a professional standpoint, mentors, bosses, clients, peers, and friends all have to be willing to speak for you in order for others to be able to trust what you say. Using this mix of references will certainly work in your favor because it's set up for answering any pertinent questions, while hopefully dispelling any doubts or concerns regarding who you are and what you can do.

When considering and being considered for an employment opportunity, be prepared and willing to interview the interviewer. An employer isn't the only one risking resources and analyzing the potential outcomes of such a commitment. You will be committing your time, talent, and intellectual value to the organization, should you receive and accept an offer. That said, you should be just as careful and concerned during the decision making process as your potential employers will be.

So, how do you interview the interviewer? Simple – by relating interviewing to sales. Now look, I know most people hate sales about as much as most people despise public speaking. However, I advise you to get the heck over it. Adapt and overcome. Whether or not you master the interviewing process can prove to be a profitable deal-maker or a disappointing deal-breaker. As one of too many candidates competing for very limited employment opportunities, we are all marketing something - our time and our skills – but very few make the actual sale.

Comparing interviewing to sales means there has to be a customer, and that customer is the potential employer. You have the challenging task of convincing your target customer that your time, which is your product, and your skills, which is your service, are the absolute best buying option in regards to return-on-investment. Here's how to transform routine interviews into deal-sealing sales meetings:

Conduct "Customer Discovery"

Simply put, do your research beforehand, take detailed notes, and commit key information to memory. Know what your customer (the potential employer) needs, and understand their mindset. What problems are persisting for them? How can you come in and help solve those problems?

Prior to your face-to-face or video-conference interview, utilize LinkedIn to find people that already work at the organization or who have worked there in the past. Initiate conversations with them through a brief invitation to connect on LinkedIn. Be upfront, and let them know you're a candidate in the running for a position at the organization of interest.

If they respond and accept your invitation, then take the liberty to ASK QUESTIONS! Do not bombard them with a laundry list of questions. Instead, spread the questions out across the various new contacts, and ask each of them one to three simple questions, such as:

- How's the workplace culture – healthy or toxic?
- How many interview rounds did you have to get through?
- How long was the hiring process before you actually started your first day of work?
- Is the team diverse?
- Would you say the organization puts its people first, or profit first?

These are some key things to discover before even considering making your sales pitch. This step in the process basically helps you qualify or disqualify a potential employer by determining how real and how desirable the opportunity actually is to you.

Rehearse Your Pitch

Practice makes improvement, and repetition builds your confidence through the reassurance of muscle-memory. Pretend like you're rehearsing to land a part in your favorite television show or something, just to liven it up a bit. You want strong, positive energy, and an assertive presence. Having your pitch perfected ahead of time empowers you, and enables you the chance to take control of the room.

Distinguish Yourself from Your Competition

Ask yourself this – why should you be hired over the countless other candidates that are clogging up the hiring pipeline? Do yourself a big favor, and refrain from lazy remarks like, "I'm the hardest worker you'll ever meet". Really? (Shaking my head) – because, as a well experienced interviewer and hiring decision maker, that's exactly what I'll do, shake my head, as I notate your lack of energy and enthusiasm for the position. Be more specific and intriguing, with statements such as: I saved my recent employer $800,000 last year by overhauling the inventory management procedures and integrating a new logistics software; or, I won employee of the month three times because of my dedication to accomplishing the mission with a great attitude every day.

Anticipate Objections and Prepare Responses

The job market can be volatile, and hiring teams can grow very apathetic through the unrelenting waves of mostly unqualified and uninteresting candidates they deal with. That's why you should expect some level of pushback, and be prepared to counteract it. Don't let the moment escape you without a valiant effort to end the customer's search. Convince them that you are the right buy, and that there's no need to look elsewhere or to entertain any other offers. Give them certainty where they have doubts, and provide clarity where any confusion exists.

Ask for the Job = Close the Sale

If the interview rounds go well, do NOT walk away from the customer without asking them to close the sale! Of course, in this context, you're asking for the job outright. Try closing with "I'm ready to start as early as Monday (*or whatever specific date you may have*). What actions do you need from me in order for us to move forward?"

If they are hesitant to make an on-the-spot commitment, then be sure to get from them a definite time and date by which you will receive their final decision. Your time is just as valuable as theirs, so there's no need to waste any on either side.

If your resume consistently gets you in the door, yet you're still in the hunt for employment, then applying the above sales strategies to your interviews should prove to be a timely solution. Once you grasp the concepts and become more comfortable as a sales person, then interviewing will truly become an uncomplicated process for you. Interviewing = Sales, and Sales = $$$,$$$.$$

If you don't know it already, please understand that compensation negotiations begin before you ever walk in the door for an interview. It begins with the company's predetermined salary range budget. The key word there is range, which means that there is always wiggle room in the figures, so I advise you to always attempt to negotiate at least once before accepting any offer. If you'd like to chat more about salary negotiations, feel free to book a brief call with me through my Calendly link -> https://calendly.com/fortiphi (for FREE).

When in need of new connections, you should first tap into your existing network. Ask yourself:

- What cross-functional allies do you already have?
- Who can you invite out for coffee or tea?
- Who in your network is in a position to coordinate an informational interview for you?

If you're a military veteran, you should strongly consider getting yourself a mentor in the civilian sector who can relate to your military background and transition. The best way to do so is to join Veterati (https://www.veterati.com/).

Do What You Can With What You Have

My brother and I, both college graduates and both with significant leadership experience, have each endured a stretch of frustrating and uncomfortable unemployment, despite our education and work history. We are not strangers to the occasional hardship, and working hard for not much is no new concept to us. Growing up, we always found ways to make honest money: sweeping up the local barbershop and passing out their flyers; mowing grass; shoveling snow; helping people move stuff; whatever we could get into. By the time I was thirteen I had a part-time job at a fast-food restaurant, and never went without a paycheck until my transition from active duty military a few years back.

We grew up in a modest household, and most of what we worked for wasn't just money for the mall and movies, although we did enjoy our fair share of leisure. We helped alleviate economic pressures from our mother by purchasing some of our own school clothes, shoes, supplies, and even helping pay a few bills from time to time. That being said, we learned the value of a dollar and strong work ethic very early in life. *We were always taught to do what we can with what we have.*

During my personal career transition journey, I needed suits and civilian work attire desperately. I spent seven years on active duty in the United States Air Force, so I was used to wearing a uniform to work every day. I did purchase two custom suits during my tour in South Korea, but by the time I needed to wear them for the many dozens (felt more like hundreds) of interviews I ended up doing over the nearly two years of transition, I couldn't fit them as well. I needed bigger jackets, bigger slacks, bigger shirts, and at least one pair of dress shoes that weren't military-issued black low-quarters. But there was the problematic fact that my pockets hadn't gotten any bigger. In fact, they'd gotten a lot smaller. My cash flow was super low, but I knew I had to improve my look along with everything else I was working to improve, regardless.

After a few discussions with my brother, we came up with a solution that turned out so much better than we ever expected. Today we call it "GOODWILL Hunting". Yes, I know that's the title of a hit movie that starred a young Matt Damon, Ben Affleck, and Robin Williams. But I'm not talking about films here. I mean hunting for quality threads at your local Goodwill. Hey, no shame in my game about it either. In fact, I make a heck of a lot more money today, but I still browse and patronize my local Goodwill from time to time. They have deals you can't refuse!

In all honesty though, my first trip to Goodwill had me doing a stroll of shame through the parking lot on my way to the entrance. I thought to myself, "what the f*%k happened to you man?" As anti-pop culture as I've always been, I'd be lying if I said I wasn't trying to maintain a certain status and appearance through my state of adversity at the time. And honestly, keeping up appearances is an unfortunately vital factor of conquering your transition. However, you can and should sustain your appearance affordably, especially if you've got dependents like I do. Every dollar and cent has to stretch in hard times. GOODWILL Hunting is the way to go.

For less than $200, my first GOODWILL Hunting trip resulted in five suit jackets, two pairs of khakis, two pairs of dress slacks, and ten non-defective button-up shirts. Name brand recognition is not a priority on my list of lifestyle choices, but know that I bought quality threads from high-end brands for literally dirt cheap! I'm talking about Saks Fifth Avenue, Dockers, Calvin Klein, Express, and more. I walked in with a low countenance, and walked out with renewed encouragement. That would've easily cost me a couple thousand dollars brand new at retail, but I paid less than $200! So, I cruised right on over to the dry cleaners up the block, for some miscellaneous alterations and some service to make gently used garments fresh and new again. If your pockets are light at the moment, I highly encourage you to do the same.

GRIND

EMBRACE "THE SUCK"

Career transition is a rowdy contender, but it can be neutralized, subdued, and conquered. Imagine you are carrying a two-edged sword. You can either choose to fall on that sword and give up, or you can choose to wield the sword properly, both for offensive and defensive purposes. What the heck am I talking about now, right?

On one edge of the sword is whatever label sticks to you the most, and it carries stereotypes along with it. For instance, are you a millennial? Based on that label alone, people may assume you're unprepared, selfish, lazy, materialistic, unwilling to conform, feel entitled, and are less willing to put in work. Some people even say that millennials are way too concerned with "keeping it real", and that millennials should worry more about how to craft an acceptable work persona instead. Are you a woman? What if some folks view you as naturally weaker than your male coworkers? Do you fear opportunity will be withheld from you if you desire to be a mother and have a career simultaneously?

Then there's the other edge of the sword, which is another classification or categorization of you as a person in this society, and will also come along with its own set of stereotypes to overcome. Take military veterans for example – some people in the civilian world may view veterans as rigid, prideful, mentally unstable, plagued by post-traumatic stress, unable to adjust to life outside of the uniform, lacking in creativity, and unable to think outside the box.

As someone who identifies as both a millennial and as a military veteran, I hear those negative stereotypes and am ready, at any moment, to help those who misunderstand or inaccurately assume things to gain the proper perspective. I embrace "the suck" of conscious and subconscious bias, and prepare to do battle against them both daily. I advise you to do the same. We must wisely and skillfully wield our metaphorical double-edged swords that we are all carrying, to defend our credibility and to strike back with facts and truths of advantage. I want to share with you some strategies, tactics and techniques.

In the military, in martial arts, and in contact sports, we are taught that defense is paramount. Patience and resilience sets a strong base. Get in tune with your environment, decreasing the likelihood that you'll overlook a crucial opportunity. Take your time thinking and analyzing, but don't hesitate when you need to take action. When networking and interviewing, try to listen a lot more than you speak. Know when to step forward, when to stand firm, and when to take a step back during negotiations. Study your targets, so that you can plan for every possible outcome. Always draw from your strengths. If a weakness happens to get exposed, then have a positively-framed rebuttal ready. Stay focused on your primary goals, and you will not get blindsided or tricked into shifting your vision. And lastly, don't be afraid to get hit – in this context, don't be scared to make a mistake. Fear will ruin you before you even get started.

On the offense, place and hold a firm grip on your morals, values, beliefs, and goals. With a firm grip, you will throw much more effective strikes. Know what to say, when to say it, and how to say it. Seek out and ask for opportunity, then go execute with precision. Emphasize your life experience in situations where you might not have the desired amount of industry experience. Be bold, and take risks. For instance, if you read a job description that you don't necessarily meet all the requirements for, but you really want the job and know that you have the wherewithal to perform it with excellence, then go and get it. Find ways to demonstrate your creativity and ability to think outside the box. You can start a blog, launch a podcast, host some sort of relevant event, or identify a problem within an organization and pitch a solution. Make sure you're out networking when you're able to. The more folks get to know you, the more they'll speak and vouch for you when needed. Also, ask for letters of recommendation and written critiques from time to time, even if not from a supervisor or manager directly above you.

Peer reviews are awesome to collect as well. These periodic check ups will let you know how you're being perceived, and provide a document trail for you to track your progression.

You have a variety of critical competitive advantages to choose from, but only if you communicate them as such. Let nothing misrepresent you personally, or any of your groups of belonging collectively (i.e. Women, Veterans, Millennials, Blacks/African Americans, etc.). Always let your unique value be known, while also latching on to key shared attributes of your various communities.

GAS AND GROCERIES

During times of transition, circumstances may be different than when you're fully employed. For instance, you might have to live with family or friends temporarily, due to the need for reducing expenses and conserving limited resources. Regardless of your residential scenario, and no matter if you're married or single with kids or no kids, two expenses remain constant: gas and groceries.

You need gas to travel around town to interviews, job fairs, training opportunities, and networking events. If you don't have a vehicle currently, then maybe you need money to cover a bus pass, a train pass, or even Uber or Lyft rides. No matter how we slice it, transportation is a constant expected expense. Groceries are also a constant expected expense, because we all need to eat. In lieu of a full-time, steady paycheck, here are several ways to earn money that'll keep you in the hunt:

- Wonolo: download the mobile application and start working flexible shifts across a variety of industries as early as tomorrow at https://wonolo.com
- Veryable: find manufacturing and warehousing work today to earn money now at https://veryableops.com
- Handy: gain access to hundreds of jobs in your city and build your own schedule at https://handy.com
- Shipt: get paid to shop for others, earning up to $22 hourly or more at https://shipt.com

- MovingHelper.com: need work? help others move when they rent a U-Haul truck and decide they need some extra hands
- Thumbtack.com: create a profile and decide when, where, and how you want to work (for photography, furniture assembly, residential cleaning, tutoring, teaching music lessons, graphic design, and much more)

Grab a friend and start a 2-person moving crew through U-Haul's affiliate www.MovingHelper.com database. You don't need a moving truck, because one is

provided to the customer directly through U-Haul. It doesn't require moving industry experience or business insurance, you get to set your own prices, and you control the distance you're willing to travel locally to service customers. All you provide is general labor to load and/or unload moving trucks for the U-Haul customers that book your crew.

Monetize your individual skills on www.Thumbtack.com. You can grab a vacuum, mop, bucket, broom, and cleaning supplies and start booking house cleaning customers immediately. If you're the creative type, you can also monetize services such as photography, voiceover production, and more.

By the way, I've personally earned money for my own gas and groceries with each and every resource I listed above (my favorites being Handy and MovingHelper.com). Bottom line is - where there's a will, there's a way. There are some obvious resources that I skipped over: i.e. Uber, Lyft, InstaCart, UberEats, DoorDash, etc. The general public is well aware of most mega names of these brands, so I hope my list has introduced you to some fresh new options.

Becoming More Valuable

I'm a huge fan of the HGTV network, especially of the renovation shows like *Fixer Upper* and *Love It or List It*. I'm always fascinated with how a home in great shape can still be made so much better. There's often a home in a great location with a solid foundation and excellent features such as a brick fireplace, yet the layout and some of the fixtures, appliances, and overall design are outdated.

Renovations are often completed with resale value as a top priority, making sure to refresh the design to be modern while still respecting and honoring the history and unique characteristics of the home.

In some instances, we can look at ourselves as homes with equity, in need of some renovations to increase the resale value. How do we as people become more valuable like a renovated home? Well, here are some great suggestions to consider:

- Learn to speak a new language, which you can do for free using mobile applications such as https://www.duolingo.com/
- Gain skills in web development, i.e. SQL, Python, HTML, JavaScript, and more, also for free on sites like https://www.freecodecamp.org/
- For military veterans in particular, there's a great web development boot camp that's free for those accepted into the program called https://vetswhocode.io/

In this chapter we're focused on making ourselves more valuable, and becoming as close to storm-proof and bullet-proof as possible. We want our value to never depreciate, but to consistently grow instead. With that in mind, here are twelve websites with value-adding content to help you stay informed and capable of relevant conversation:

1. **FortiPhi.co**
2. **SalesHacker.com**
3. **Jopwell.com**
4. **WorkItDaily.com**
5. **UrbanGeekz.com**
6. **WomenWorking.com**
7. **BlacksInTechnology.net**
8. **USVeteransMagazine.com**
9. **BlackEOEjournal.com**
10. **CareerContessa.com**
11. **TPinsights.com (The PLUG)**
12. **DigitalNomad.com**

The job market is flooded with talented, well educated, diverse candidates, all vying for limited opportunities and resources. It is imperative to clearly differentiate yourself from your competitors and sustain high value. You need to clearly stand out from the rest of the resume pile, and then continue to separate yourself from the pack throughout the networking and interviewing processes.

GROW

Quantify and Storify

Your level of sustainable career growth possibilities rely heavily on your ability to quantify and storify. You can't just be an updated resume with fancy titles and a checklist of responsibilities. That frankly doesn't capture the attention of hiring authorities. You need to differentiate yourself and stand-out from the pack at all times. One of the strongest ways to do so is to quantify and storify.

To quantify is simply to validate your skills and capabilities with facts and numbers. For example:

- 90% placement success rate at or above on-target-earnings standard for graduated candidates
- Achieved 250% of target annual sales quota
- Generated $20M in new business revenue
- Accomplishing above 95% client retention rate year-over-year

It behooves you to learn how to turn your experience into a series of damn good and compelling short stories, which brings us to the context of what it means to storify. These are stories of brevity, yet have lasting impact on an audience. And by brevity, I mean one to two sentences maximum, only expounding on the story when specifically requested. Again, here are a few examples:

- Lead office from rank 156/156 up to 50/156 within first six months as the senior site leader
- Promoted to Director-level role after just eight months on staff, outperforming three higher-tenured internal competitors
- Spearheaded the promotion of five direct reports, all within the same calendar year

PLATFORM-BASED CAREER BUILDING

The best way to build your career now is from a specific platform, or rather within a particular ecosystem, especially in regards to the technology industry.

Salesforce is a great example of a robust platform with a growing ecosystem.

Within the realm of Salesforce exist careers for Developers, HR professionals, Account Executives, Certified Administrators, Marketing experts, Financial specialists, and more. Salesforce supports the sustainment of its ecosystem by offering continuous access to specialized training and development via their Trailhead (https://trailhead.salesforce.com/en/home), and through acquisitions of companies like Tableau, MuleSoft, and Heroku. In addition to all opportunities native to Salesforce directly, your career can benefit indirectly through Salesforce-related roles at partner organizations like Penrod, Coastal Cloud, Accenture Federal, Capgemini, Deloitte Digital, Slalom, PwC, Simplus, Pracedo, and many many more.

Other strong platforms and ecosystems to sync your career with include but are not limited to: Amazon Web Services (AWS); Microsoft; ServiceNow; Cisco; Splunk; etc.

Once You're Hired ...

When you receive the burden-lifting message of "congratulations, you're hired", the battle of the job hunt is won. However, the war of career sustainment wages on. Treat being hired as a pivot point rather than as a stopping point.

So, once you've been onboarded at your new job and have already started working for a few days, here are seven action items that will help you sustain your progress:

- **Establish a 30-60-90 Day Plan** by the end of your first week on the new job
    - What training do you need to complete?
    - What people within the organization do you need to make initial contact with?
    - What are your specific and measurable goals within your new role?

- Update your **LinkedIn** profile
    - Headline
    - Current Employer
    - Job Title and Job Description

- Update your **Resume** - get it ready for the next round with current employer, job title, role description, and start date

- Send Thank You Cards to:
  - Your References
  - Any Recruiters responsible for presenting you with the opportunity and guiding you through the hiring process
  - Family & Friends in your personal support system (spouse, kids, parents, siblings, etc.)

- Prepare an **Exit Strategy** (just as business owners should do)
  - What will you do if the company downsizes and your position gets eliminated?
  - What lateral positions could you fulfill?
  - How do you achieve the next level up?
  - What other companies/organizations are you interested in working with?

- Have a bit of **fun** with your new coworkers
  - Join the lunch crowd once or twice a week
  - Attend a company-sponsored happy hour
  - Treat someone for coffee

- Book Informational Interviews over coffee or tea - this sets you up for potential growth opportunities in the future, and gives you leverage to negotiate promotions and pay raises later

- Make friends across your industry before you need them

For continuous success, you always have to have grit and understand that the grind never stops. Never get too comfortable - it'll stunt your growth and create blind spots. Instead, welcome disruption and embrace the role of being a change-agent, starting with yourself. I hope reading this book helped you generate some epiphanies and identify many actionables for you to make good on.

Let's connect! You can find me on Twitter @lexRbrown, on LinkedIn at https://linkedin.com/in/lexRbrown and also on Instagram @lexRbrown. Oh, and checkout my website for some pretty awesome tee shirts, coffee mugs, journals, and other swag: https://fortiphi.co. I've got more great books on the way, but I'll let you finish digesting this one first. Cheers!

Resources

In this section I am dedicating a full page to each resource that I recommend you explore and consider. Although I identify who each resource is intended for, I purposely listed them in no particular order. Rather than alphabetize or categorize, I think it'd be beneficial for you to read each resource's page. If a resource doesn't benefit you specifically, maybe it will help someone you know. You can also lean on these resources when out networking to help add value to conversations when others are seeking help. If you have any resource suggestions for future book revisions, or to be considered for listing on the FortiPhi.co blog, please email me at *lex@fortiphi.co*.

Job Search Mastery Class (JSMC)

Website URL: http://jobsearchmasterclass.com/

Who is this for? U.S. Military Veterans, Transitioning Service Members, Military Spouses, and the General Public

Resource Summary: Founded by Global Career Expert, Speaker, Trainer and Forbes.com Coaches Council Member, Dana Manciagli, JSMC is a complete online job search program with everything you need to apply and interview with confidence, making yourself undeniable to employers, and landing a great job in record time. Once enrolled, you gain 24/7 access to the platform, comprehensive instructional tools, templates, and a proven system to improve the speed and quality of your job search.

There are five core modules, 20 lessons, plus over 35 checklists, cheat sheets, and templates. You'll get lifetime access to frequently updated content, and be invited to a robust and exclusive online community. You'll conduct your job search while learning throughout JSMC. The results are measurable in boosts to your number of quality interviews and job offers for roles that you actually like!

TECH QUALLED

Tech Qualled

Website URL: https://qualled.com/

Who is this for? U.S. Military Veterans and Transitioning Service Members

Resource Summary: Tech Qualled is an ideal bridge into high-tech sales careers for U.S. Military Veterans and Transitioning Service Members. Entry into Tech Qualled's Launchpad Sales Academy is very competitive and highly selective. As a result, Tech Qualled consistently achieves an 85-90% placement success rate for candidates who complete the 7-week program.

While most folks have the image of a pesky car salesman when they hear "sales career", high-tech sales is all about using technology to solve business problems. You're a consultant and trusted advisor, not just a product pusher, and will typically see a 50/50 split between your base salary and commission during the first year. Most Account Executives in high-tech sales earn a six-figure annual compensation.

MilSpo Academy

Website URL: https://milspoacademy.com/

Who is this for? Military Spouses

Resource Summary: MilSpo Academy is designed to get military spouses hired and succeeding in roles that are typically being worked remotely. Target job categories include business development, recruiting, virtual assistant, and digital marketings and social media management.

*"Find out what you like doing best
and get someone to pay you for it"*

MilSpo Academy's mission is to help as many spouses as possible find, earn, and outperform in careers that pay well, offer advancement, and provide the opportunity to work remotely.

Jopwell

Website URL: https://www.jopwell.com/

Who is this for? Black, Latinx, and Native American Students and Professionals

Resource Summary: According to Business Insider, America's leading companies like Lyft, Pinterest, Pfizer, and even the NBA, among others, have partnered with Jopwell to more easily connect with minorities.

Representation matters, so Jopwell serves as a career advancement platform for Black, Latinx, and Native American students and professionals. They also assist companies directly with their diversity recruitment, marketing, and retention efforts at scale.

Jopwell also has an excellent blog called "The WELL" (https://jopwell.com/thewell) with amazing career advice, news on diversity, and other premium content.

Work It Daily

Website URL: https://www.workitdaily.com/

Who is this for? Under-Employed and Dissatisfied Professionals

Resource Summary: WorkItDaily will help you up your career game. I've been personally following WorkItDaily since it was CAREEREALISM, and it's Founder J.T. O'Donnell, who is an elite career-growth sage. WorkItDaily's mantra is that "it's your career and you should love it". You can get help from trained career coaches with everything resumes and cover letters to negotiating compensation packages.

#VetsWhoCode

Vets Who Code

Website URL: https://vetswhocode.io/

Who is this for? U.S. Military Veterans seeking careers in web development and software engineering roles

Resource Summary: Vets Who Code is a veteran-led and operated 501(c)(3) charitable nonprofit that focuses on training veterans in web development and software engineering principles, FREE of charge, with the focus on starting careers as JavaScript Developers. Yes, it is FREE, but entry is very competitive and selective for each cohort.

I helped co-found this organization back in 2014, when it began simply as FRAGO. Jerome Hardaway is the primary Founder and still Vets Who Code's principle leader. Seek him out on LinkedIn if you'd like to learn more: https://www.linkedin.com/in/jerome-hardaway/.

Veterati

Website URL: https://www.veterati.com/

Who is this for? Mentoring Network for the Military Community

Resource Summary: Join thousands of Service Members, Veterans, and Military Spouses in setting up free one-hour mentorship phone calls with successful professionals. Veterati is the only Veteran Mentorship Platform to let you choose your own mentors and as many as you would like. The average member selects around four mentors, and some mentees have 25+ mentors! You can create a FREE profile at Veterati to get unlimited access to thousands of volunteer mentors: CEOs, recruiters, entrepreneurs, managers, fellow Veterans and civilians alike.

I've been a Veterati Mentor since early 2020. Feel free to connect with me directly on the Veterati platform: https://go.veterati.com/9mY9Ul

Women Working

Website URL: https://www.womenworking.com/

Who is this for? Women and Girls Around the World

Resource Summary: Join this network to connect with like-minded women and to get exclusive updates, bonus content, and their "Monthly Motivation" newsletter. WomenWorking.com is founded by Helene Lerner, who is an author and Emmy Award-Winning television producer. She also happens to have an MBA from Pace University, and is well-versed in the things that professional women endure everyday.

career contessa

Career Contessa

Website URL: https://www.careercontessa.com/

Who is this for? Women building careers on their terms

Resource Summary: Career Contessa offers women resources for every career stage and learning style. Their core offering is a 28-Day Career Kickstart that provides an introduction to all the ways they're helping women build successful careers. Career Contessa essentially has a four-step process: Choose a Track; Get Curated Advice; Do Your Homework; and then Earn Bonuses. Visit their website for more details.

Black EOE Journal

Website URL: https://blackeoejournal.com/

Who is this for? The African-American Community

Resource Summary: A byproduct of DiversityComm, Black EOE Journal is available electronically and in print. It's an amazing source of useful information and inspiration for both career development and entrepreneurial pursuits. Enjoy career, business, education, lifestyle and African-American role model news delivered straight to your inbox each month! Nationwide conferences, events, business and hiring expos are also featured. These events will connect you with corporations and schools looking to hire and recruit. Many of these events offer opportunities to meet face-to-face with representatives looking to do business with you! Join the Black EOE Journal community today!

Merivis

Website URL: https://merivis.org/

Who is this for? U.S. Military Veterans, Transitioning Service Members, and Military Spouses

Resource Summary: Merivis supports veterans preparing for their next mission through training, mentorship and job readiness for Salesforce cloud technology careers. They're transforming military years into rewarding tech careers. The name Merivis comes from the Latin roots of Merit and Force, a nod to both the military and business communities being served. The organization has grown into a nationwide community with a vision to open the world of cloud technology through job training, mentorship and placement for veterans everywhere.

Vetforce by Salesforce

Website URL: https://veterans.force.com/s/

Who is this for? U.S. Military Veterans and Transitioning Service Members

Resource Summary: Through Vetforce, Salesforce is committed to upskilling the military community with high demand technology skills and providing its partners with a diverse and trained talent pipeline. The Trailhead Military program via Vetforce is virtual, self-paced, FREE, and can be started in minutes. You're not just joining a training program, you're joining a tight knit community of over 30,000 members focused on career success.

AWS Educate

Website URL: https://aws.amazon.com/education/awseducate/

Who is this for? The General Public (Any and Everybody!)

Resource Summary: AWS Educate is used in more than 200 countries and territories. It connects 2,400 institutions, over 10,000 educators, and hundreds of thousands of students. Through AWS Educate, students and educators have access to content and programs developed to skill up for cloud careers in growing fields. AWS Educate also connects companies hiring for cloud skills to qualified student job seekers with the AWS Educate Job Board.

Explore Cloud Career Pathways to learn the top cloud skills in leading cloud careers. From Machine Learning Scientist to Application Developer, each pathway aligns to a specific job role and includes 25+ hours of self-paced content with knowledge checks. Earn credentials for completed pathways to share with prospective employers on the AWS Educate Job Board.

DoD SkillBridge

Website URL: https://dodskillbridge.usalearning.gov/

Who is this for? U.S. Military Service Members within 180 Days of Transition

Resource Summary: SkillBridge is an excellent opportunity as you plan for your life after the military. SkillBridge matches civilian opportunities to your job training and work experience at the end of your military duty. In addition to opportunities such as Tuition Assistance and the GI Bill program, you can enhance your marketability and post-separation career prospects by participating in a SkillBridge opportunity.

Any rank, enlisted or officer, may apply for SkillBridge. SkillBridge permits you to use up to the last 180 days of Service to train and learn with an industry partner. During SkillBridge participation you continue to receive military compensation and you are covered by your military benefits.

HireMilitary

Website URL: https://www.hiremilitary.us/

Who is this for? Transitioning U.S. Military Service Members

Resource Summary: www.HireMilitary.us (owned by TENOVA LLC) is a cloud-based platform that supports service members throughout the entire transition life-cycle. By partnering with trusted non-profits, sharing information and leveraging technology, they are able to connect service members of all ranks with employers for:

- DoD Skillbridge (Career Skills Program) training or internships
- Employment via their proprietary job board and mobile apps
- Tech-enabled hiring events (held on military installations)

They're a nation-wide network of passionate veteran and industry leaders with one goal in mind: to decrease veteran unemployment and underemployment by bringing employers and transitioning service members together.

Urban Geekz

Website URL: https://UrbanGeekz.com

Who is this for? African-American, Latinx, and Multicultural Professionals

Resource Summary: UrbanGeekz is a groundbreaking video-centric African American, Latinx, and multicultural digital news platform focused on technology, business, science, and startups. The first-of-its-kind online publication also provides authoritative lifestyle and entertainment content. UrbanGeekz was launched by winning BBC-trained journalist turned entrepreneur Kunbi Tinuoye.

CYBRARY
Cyber Security & IT Learning

Cybrary

Website URL: https://cybrary.it

Who is this for? Any and Everyone with career interests in IT and Cyber Security

Resource Summary: Cybrary puts the collective knowledge of top subject matter experts and leading organizations in the cybersecurity industry at your fingertips. Its ever-growing network enables them to move quickly with emerging trends and new technologies to deliver timely, quality content, tools, and resources. Cybrary leverages its partnerships to provide a myriad of learning opportunities to develop your cybersecurity skills and help you achieve your career goals. Cybrary provides cybersecurity training classes to everyone, everywhere! Get started growing your skill set today and become part of their education revolution!

Free Code Camp

Website URL: https://www.freecodecamp.org/

Who is this for? Any and Everyone who wants to Learn to Code

Resource Summary: Since 2014, more than 40,000 freeCode Camp.org graduates have gotten jobs at tech companies like Apple, Google, Microsoft, Spotify, and Amazon. You can earn FREE, verified certifications in a myriad of specialties and focus areas such as: Data Visualization; Responsive Web Design; Quality Assurance; Information Security; Machine Learning; and more. Learn SQL, Python, JavaScript, HTML, and much more for free!

Quick Start

Website URL: https://www.quickstart.com/

Who is this for? Any and Everyone interested in IT Careers

Resource Summary: QuickStart offers IT certifications online to help you achieve career growth and IT workforce readiness via artificial intelligence (A.I.) and virtual-instructor led training. Not a newcomer to IT? QuickStart's programs can help you get promoted and increase your overall income. Checkout their website for more details. If asked or prompted about how you heard about them, please tell them that Lex Brown from Tech Qualled sent you :)

Blendoor

Website URL: https://www.blendoor.com/

Who is this for? Job Seekers with Diverse Cultures and Backgrounds

Resource Summary: You can utilize Blendoor to find opportunities and firms where you're most likely to belong and succeed based on your identity, experiences, and core values. According to Glassdoor: 76% of job seekers and employees today report that a diverse workforce is an important factor when evaluating companies and job offers. Job Seekers increasingly want to work for companies that effectively balance people, planet and profitability, and Blendoor helps to bring clarity and equity in that regard.

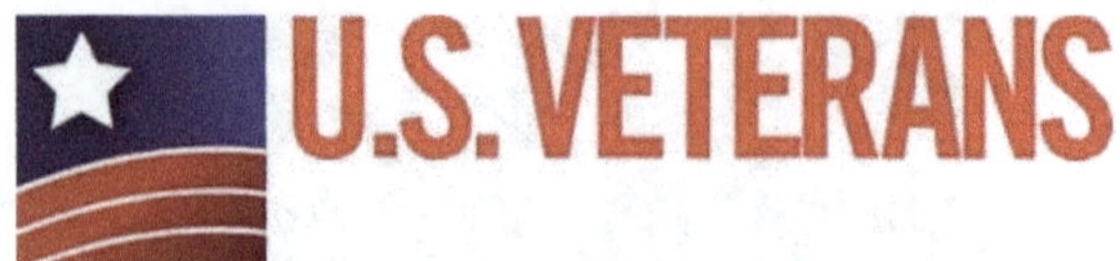

US Veterans Magazine

Website URL: https://usveteransmagazine.com/

Who is this for? The Military Community

Resource Summary: Another great byproduct of DiversityComm, US Veterans Magazine is a quarterly publication available electronically and in print. It's essentially a resource that provides educational, career and business insight. It opens up immediate lucrative employment, business and supplier opportunities for veterans, transitioning service members, disabled veterans and veteran business owners within the Federal Government as well as Corporate America.

Hispanic Network Magazine

Website URL: https://hnmagazine.com/

Who is this for? The Latinx Community

Resource Summary: Yes, yet another great byproduct of Diversity-Comm, and a premier source for employment and business opportunities targeting #Hispanics, #Latinx and Native Americans. It is available electronically and in print. HISPANIC Network Magazine has created an environment for Hispanics to acquire business knowledge and unlock career opportunities. It strives to bring promising, talented people together with potential employers and customers throughout the business community. HISPANIC Network Magazine provides the latest and most important news spanning every industry, business and profession. This includes up-to-date statistics on workforce diversity, B2B trends, noteworthy conferences, business opportunities and role model spotlights.

Blacks in Technology

Website URL: https://www.blacksintechnology.net/

Who is this for? Black Professionals in the World of Technology

Resource Summary: Blacks in Technology is "Stomping the Divide" by delivering the most relevant and beneficial information and network for African Americans in the technology field or pursuing a career in Technology. The focus is on creating a community in which African Americans are comfortable, motivated and inspired to pursue careers in Technology. The intent is also to establish effective communication between African Americans in order to help drive individual growth, development and long-term success in the field of Technology.

Professional Woman's Magazine

Website URL: https://professionalwomanmag.com/

Who is this for? Professional Women

Resource Summary: Professional Woman's Magazine is dedicated to promoting the advancement of multicultural, diverse women in all aspects of business and employment to ensure equal opportunity. It covers news information ranging from professional concerns to civic affairs, trends, careers and business, life-style issues, the arts, education, finance, health, technology, family, travel all of which impact a professional woman. Oh, and this publication, another offspring of DiversityComm, is available electronically as well as in print.

DIVERSEability Magazine

Website URL: https://diverseabilitymagazine.com/

Who is this for? People with All Types of Disabilities

Resource Summary: DIVERSEability is a diversity and inclusion magazine featuring individuals with all types of diverse abilities. It's more than just a magazine raising awareness and providing educational, employment and business opportunities - it's a movement celebrating advancements and achievements that inspires the world. It is available electronically and in print.

www.ingramcontent.com/pod-product-compliance
Lightning Source LLC
Chambersburg PA
CBHW051006050726
47592CB00007B/2731